# Doctor Knickerbocker
## and Other Rhymes

A CANADIAN COLLECTION

Kids Can Press Ltd. acknowledges with appreciation the assistance of
the Canada Council and the Ontario Arts Council in the production of this book.

Canadian Cataloguing in Publication Data
Main entry under title:

Doctor Knickerbocker and other rhymes : a Canadian collection

Includes bibliographical references and index.
ISBN 1-55074-079-2 (bound)  ISBN 1-55074-253-1 (pbk.)

1. Counting-out rhymes — Canada.  2. Children's songs — Canada.  3. Nursery rhymes, English.
I. Booth, David.  II. Kovalski, Maryann.
GR480.D64  1993      j398.8'0971      C92-095131-7

Kids Can Press Ltd.
29 Birch Avenue
Toronto, Ontario, Canada
M4V 1E2

Printed and bound in Hong Kong
PA 95  0 9 8 7 6 5 4 3 2 1

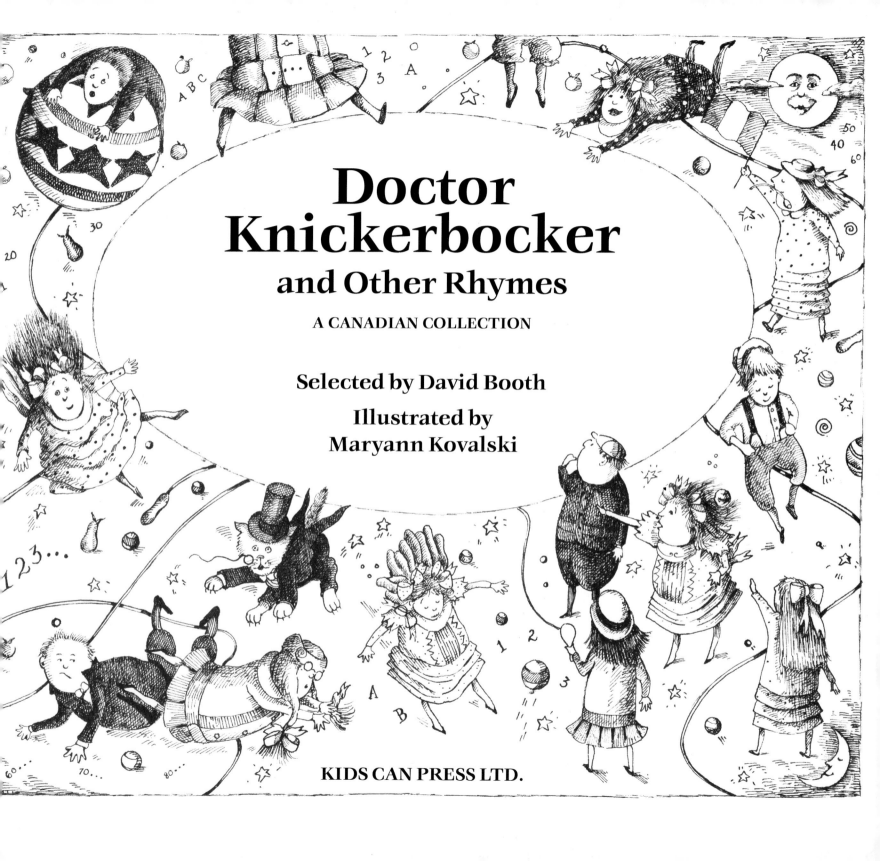

# Doctor Knickerbocker
## and Other Rhymes

A CANADIAN COLLECTION

**Selected by David Booth**

**Illustrated by**
**Maryann Kovalski**

KIDS CAN PRESS LTD.

For Michael Hermiston

D.B.

For Joanna

M.K.

I wish to thank Larry Swartz and his grade five students
at Queenston Drive Public School for their help in discovering
all the rhymes on their playground.
And Marion Seary, for reading the manuscript and offering
such helpful suggestions.

D.B.

# Contents

Introduction  vi

OUT LOUD, RIGHT NOW!  1
Contemporary schoolyard rhymes

MAMA SAID IT AND I SAY IT TOO  21
Schoolyard rhymes from yesterday still heard today

ECHOES FROM LONG AGO  51
Remembering a century of schoolyard rhymes

Other Collections of Schoolyard Rhymes  68

Index of First Lines  69

Index of Rhymes by Type  70

# Introduction

When my son Jay came home from camp, I heard him singing

Miss Mary Mack, Mack, Mack,
Dressed in black, black, black,
With silver buttons, buttons, buttons,
Down her back, back, back.

I asked him where he learned the rhyme. "From the big girls at the back of the bus!" he replied. And thus *Doctor Knickerbocker and Other Rhymes* was born. Together, we began to collect these verses from the literature of childhood. They spilled out on the way to school, during recess, on the bus, after four, as well as from the books we had collected — all part

of the wit and wisdom of the young.

We heard chants, skipping rhymes, jingles, riddles, sayings and superstitions, taunts and teases, catcalls and retorts, autograph verses, street songs, counting-out rhymes, ball-bounce chants, tongue twisters, join-in rhythms, action songs, nonsense verses, lullabies, jokes, silly rhymes, ruderies, nicknames, slogans and ads, and memory gems gathered from long-ago voices — all shouted and sung in the freedom of the playground. These verses form the folk poetry of childhood.

Contemporary rhymes are celebrated in the first

section of the book, "Out Loud, Right Now!" You may recognize a phrase from a television show, a tune from an advertisement, a line from a cartoon, a rhyme from a song. You'll hear a rude expression for an enemy, a city with a great-sounding name, an alphabet rhyme for choosing who is first, a counting verse for deciding who is last, a friend's name (or even your own) made into a rhyme. And, like magic, these creations alter overnight, springing up anew on an unsuspecting playground in some other city.

The verses in "Mama Said It and I Say It Too" really belong to your parents. Some of the names and words may not make much sense now, but your parents and teachers will remember them and be able to tell you their origins. Whether they were first called out by your mother or your father or your uncle Jack, the words are here so you can call them out one more time.

"Echoes from Long Ago" includes verses from your grandparents' time, verses from childhoods in England, Scotland, Ireland, Wales and North America. When people emigrated to North America from all over the world, they brought with them very few possessions, but all kinds of memories. And the children, just like you, added their voices to the streets and schoolyards of their new homes. What a surprise to find some of their words still shouted and sung today! Other rhymes have faded into the past, but when we see the verses written down, we can imagine the echoes of children's voices from many, many years ago.

Had a little sports car 298,
And I ran around a corner
And I slammed on the brakes.
 I bumped into a lady,
  I bumped into a man,
  I bumped into a policeman,
  Man oh man!

  Policeman caught me , put me in jail,
  All I had was ginger ale.
  How many bottles did I have?
  1, 2, 3, 4 ...

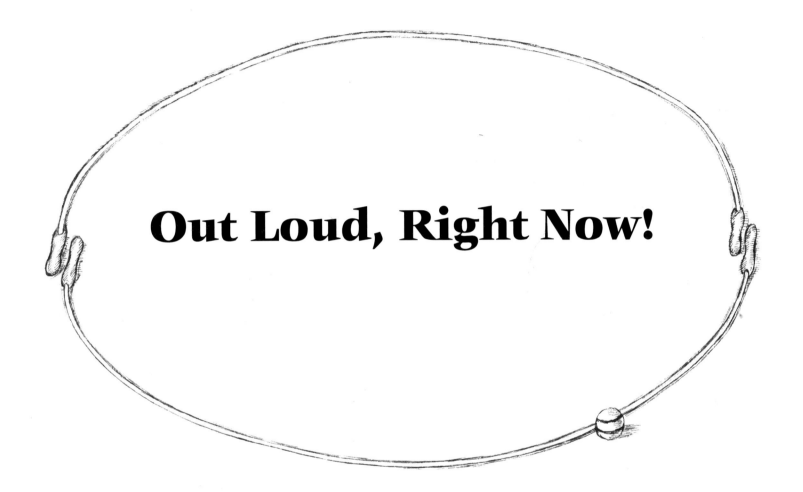

# Out Loud, Right Now!

2

slowly, I crunch them very fast. I never eat the chocolate, I always eat the shell. When I eat my Smarties, I eat them very well.

Peter, Peter, if you're able,
Get your elbows off the table.
This is not a horse's stable,
But a ritzy dining table.

4

Doctor Knickerbocker, Knickerbocker, number nine,
I just got back and I'm feeling fine.

So let's hear the rhythm of the head, ding dong.

Now we got the rhythm of the head,
So let's hear the rhythm of the feet, stomp, stomp.

Now we got the rhythm of the feet,
So let's hear the rhythm of the hands, clap, clap.

Now we got the rhythm of the hands ...

Doctor Knickerbocker, Knickerbocker, number nine,
I just got back and I'm feeling fine.

Hot-cross buns, Hot-cross buns, One-a-penny, Two-a-penny, Hot-cross buns.

I woke up Sunday morning
And looked upon the wall.
The bedbugs and the beetles
Were having a game of ball.

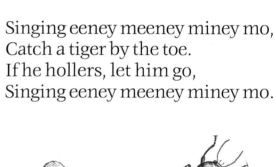

The score was six to seven,
The beetles were ahead.
The beetles hit a home run,
And knocked me out of bed.

Singing eeney meeney miney mo,
Catch a tiger by the toe.
If he hollers, let him go,
Singing eeney meeney miney mo.

**Who ate a bun? You are the one.**

March, April, May,

June, July, August, September,

October, November, December!

Billy gave me apples,
Billy gave me pears,
Billy gave me fifty cents
And kissed me on the stairs.

I gave him back his apples,
I gave him back his pears,
I gave him back his fifty cents
And kicked him down the stairs.

1, 2, 3, 4...

Hot potato,
pass it on,
pass it on, pass it on.
Who's got the hot
potato?

And this is what she sent me for:

Salt ... Vinegar ... Pepper!

9

10

Old John Tucker was a mighty man,
He washed his face in a frying pan,
He combed his hair with a wagon wheel,
And had a toothache in his heel.
So get out of the way, old John Tucker,
You're too late to get your supper.

*Charley went over the ocean,*
*Charley went over the sea.*
*Charley caught a codfish —*
*You can't catch me!*

Over the lake,
Over the sea,
Over the ocean blue.

Up the river,
Down the river,
Out goes you!

*Hickory, dickory,*
*Six and seven,*
*Abalonee, crack-a-bonee,*
*Ten and eleven,*
*Spin, spun, muskadit,*
*Ninety-nine, you are it!*

Hey, Peter!
 I think I hear my name.
Hey, Peter!
 I think I hear it again.
You're wanted on the telephone!
 If it's not Greg, then I'm not home.

Hey, Greg!
 I think I hear my name.
Hey, Greg!
 I think I hear it again.
You're wanted on the telephone!
 If it's not Jim, then I'm not home.

Hey, Jim!
 I think I hear my name ...

*Eeka locka
Horse's caca
Eeka locka
Out!*

One, two, three, four,
Mary at the cottage door.
Five, six, seven, eight,
Eating cherries off a plate.
O - U - T spells out.

13

My boyfriend's name is Addie,
He comes from Cincinnati,
With a pickle up his nose
And fourteen toes
And this is how the story goes.

While I was out there walking,
I heard my boyfriend talking
To a pretty little girl
With chocolate curls.
And this is what he said to her...
"I l-o-v-e love you,
I ki-s-s kiss you."
He jumped into the lake
And swallowed a snake,
And went home
with a bellyache.

A E I O **U**

LA BANDERA
**DE PERU**

The wonder ball
Goes round and round.
Pass it quickly
Or you'll be bound.
If you're the one
To hold it last,
Then for you
This game is past.
YOU ARE OUT!

Miss Mary had a steamboat,

The [steamboat] had a [bell],

Ding, ding!

Miss Mary went to [heaven],

The steamboat went to ...

Hello operator,

Please give me number 9,

And if you disconnect me,

I'll [kick] your ...

Behind the yellow [curtains],

There was a piece of [toilet roll].

Miss Mary [sat] upon it

And poked her little ...

Ask me no more ? ? ?,

Please tell me no more lies,

The [boys] are in the [bathroom]

Doing up their ...

The [flies] are in the [city],

The [ants] are in the [park],

Miss Mary and her boyfriend

Are [kiss]ing in the dark dark dark.

Row, row, row your boat gently down the stream.

Up on the housetop,
reindeer pause,
Out jumps good old
Santa Claus,
Down through the chimney
with lots of toys,
All for the little ones –
Christmas joys.

Jingle bells,
Batman smells,
Robin laid an egg.
The Batmobile lost a wheel,
And the Joker took ballet.
Hey!

Tom, Tom, the piper's son, Went to school with nothing on

Teacher said, "That's not fair! Give me back my underwear."

I went into the house.
*Just like me.*
I went upstairs.
*Just like me.*
I went into a room.
*Just like me.*
I looked in the glass.
*Just like me.*
I saw a monkey.
*Just like me.*

# Mama Said It and I Say It Too

Postman,
postman,
Do your duty.
Send this letter
To my cutie.
Don't you stop
Nor don't delay.
Get it to her
Right away.

If you think you
are in love,
And still there
is some question,

Don't worry much
about it,
It may be
indigestion.

When you
fall in the river
There is a boat,
When you fall in the well
There is a rope,
When you fall in love
There is no
hope.

CARTER'S
LITTLE
LIVER
PILLS
TRADE MARK

Vegetable Love,
Do you carrot all for me?
My heart beets for you.
With your turnip nose
And your radish face,
You are a peach.
If we cantaloupe,
Lettuce marry;
Weed make a swell pear.

When you see a monkey up a tree,
Pull on his tail and think of me.

Roses are red,
    Violets are blue,

What you need
    Is a good shampoo.

Through the teeth,
Past the gums,
Look out, stomach,
Here it comes!

Mind your own business
And don't mind mine.
Kiss your own sweetheart
And don't kiss mine.

I saw you in the ocean,
I saw you in the sea,
I saw you in the bathtub,
Oops! Pardon me!

When you get married
And your wife has twins,
Just call on me for safety pins.

Tarzan, Tarzan, in the air,
Tarzan lost his underwear.
Tarzan say, "Me no care.
Me no wear no underwear!"

Mary had a little lamb,
Its fleece was white as snow,
And everywhere that Mary went,
—She took it on a bus.

Mary had a little lamb,
Her father shot it dead.
And now it goes to school with her
Between two chunks of bread.

26

*Mary had a little lamb,*
*It was a greedy glutton.*
*She fed it ice-cream all day long,*
*And now it's frozen mutton.*

*Mary had a little lamb,*
*You've heard this tale before,*
*But did you know she passed her plate*
*And had a little more?*

Mary had a little cow,
It fed on safety pins.
And every time she milked the cow,
The milk came out in tins.

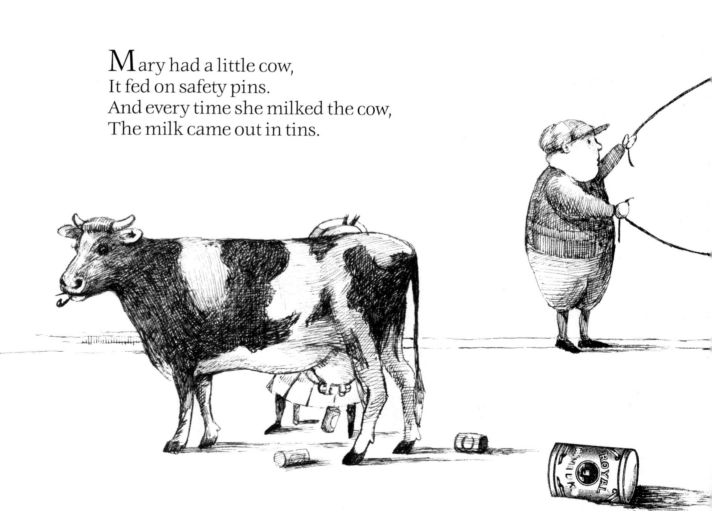

Way down south where bananas grow, A grasshopper stepped on an elephant's toe. The elephant said, with tears in his eyes, "Pick on someone more your own size."

28

The funniest thing I've ever seen
Was a tomcat sewing on a sewing machine.
Oh, the sewing machine got running too slow,
And it took seven stitches in the tomcat's toe.

Mother, may I take a swim?

Yes, my darling daughter,
But hang your clothes on a
hickory limb,
And don't go near the water.

What's the time? Time you bought a watch!

The same time as it was this time yesterday.

What's the time? About now.

What's the time? Ten o'clock next Wednesday.

A minute to the next.

Time you knew better. What's the time?

What's the time? What's the time? time?

Half past, quarter to strike, ten minutes to the lamp-post. What's the

What's the time? Half past kissing time and time to kiss again.

Who stole the cookie from the cookie jar?

Nancy stole the cookie from the cookie jar.

Who, me?

Yes, you.

Couldn't be!

Then who?

Jenny stole the cookie from the cookie jar.

Who, me?

Yes, you.

Couldn't be!

The w

Charlie Chaplin
   went to France
To teach the pretty girls
   to dance.
First one heel,
   Then the toe,
   Do the splits
      And around you go.
      Salute to the captain,
         Curtsey to the queen,
         Touch the bottom
            of the submarine.

31

Are you coming out, sir?
No, sir.
Why, sir?
Because I've got a cold, sir.
Where'd you get the cold, sir?
At the North Pole, sir.
What were you doing there, sir?
Catching polar bears, sir.
How many did you catch, sir?
One, sir, two, sir, three, sir,
That's enough for me, sir.

Eenie, meenie, minie, mo.
Catch a tiger by the toe;
If he hollers make him pay
Fifty dollars every day.
Out goes Y-O-U!

This is the way you spell Tennessee. One asee, two asee, three asee, four asee,

Monkey in the jailhouse,
Don't you hear him holler?
Took a pickle from a fish,
And didn't pay a dollar.
One, two, three,
Out goes she.

Fireman, fireman, number eight,
Hit his head against the gate.
The gate flew in, the gate flew out,
That's the way he put the fire out.
O-U-T spells out,
And out you go.

*five asee, six asee, seven asee,* *eight asee, nine asee, Tennessee!*

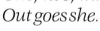

The elephant is a pretty bird,
It flits from bough to bough.
It builds its nest in a rhubarb tree,
And whistles like a cow.

Ladies and gentlemen, take my advice, pull down your pants and slide on the ice.

Nobody likes me, everybody hates me,
Guess I'll eat some worms.
Itsy-bitsy tiny ones,
Slippy, slurpy, grimy ones,
Look at those little things squirm.

First one was easy,
Second one was greasy,
Third one got stuck in my throat.
Hasten, Jason, call Dr. Mason,
Get these ghastly things out!

WELCOME MAMAS AND PAPAS
A fly and a flea flew up in a flue. Said the fly to the flea, "What shall we do?" "Let's fly," said the flea. "Let's flee," said the fly. So they flew up a flaw in the flue.
How much wood would a woodchuck chuck If a woodchuck could chuck wood? He would chuck what wood a woodchuck could chuck If a woodchuck could chuck wood.
If Peter Piper picked a peck of pickled peppers, A peck of pickled peppers Peter Piper picked. But if Peter Piper picked a peck of pickled peppers, Where is the peck of pickled peppers Peter Piper picked?

Popeye the sailor man, He lived in a caravan. He opened the door

Salome was a dancer,
She danced before the king.
She danced the hanky-panky,
And she shimmied everything.
The king said, "Salome,
You can't do that in here!"
Salome said, "Baloney!"
And kicked the chandelier.

My boy-friend gave me peaches,
My boy-friend gave me pears,
My boy-friend gave me fifty cents
To fix the broken stairs.

My mother ate the peaches,
My brother ate the pears,
My father ate the fifty cents
And fell right down the stairs.

My mother gave me a nickel,
My father gave me a dime,
My sister gave me a lover boy
That kissed me all the time.

My mother took my nickel,
My father took my dime,
My sister took my lover boy
And gave me Frankenstein.

He made me wash the dishes,
He made me scrub the floor,
But I didn't like that a single bit,
So I kicked him out the door.

I'm Chiquita Banana, and I'm here to say, If you want to get rid of your teacher today, Just peel a banana, put it on the floor, And watch your teacher slide out the door.
Up the river, Down the lake, Teacher's got The stomach-ache.
Four more days and we are free From the school of misery. No more pencils, no more books, No more teacher's sassy looks.
Tonight, tonight, the pillow fight, Tomorrow's the end of school. Break the dishes, break the chairs, Trip the teacher on the stairs.

47

One for sorrow, two for joy,
Three for a kiss and four for a boy,
Five for silver, six for gold,
Seven for a secret never to be told.
Eight for a letter from over the sea,
Nine for a lover as true as can be.

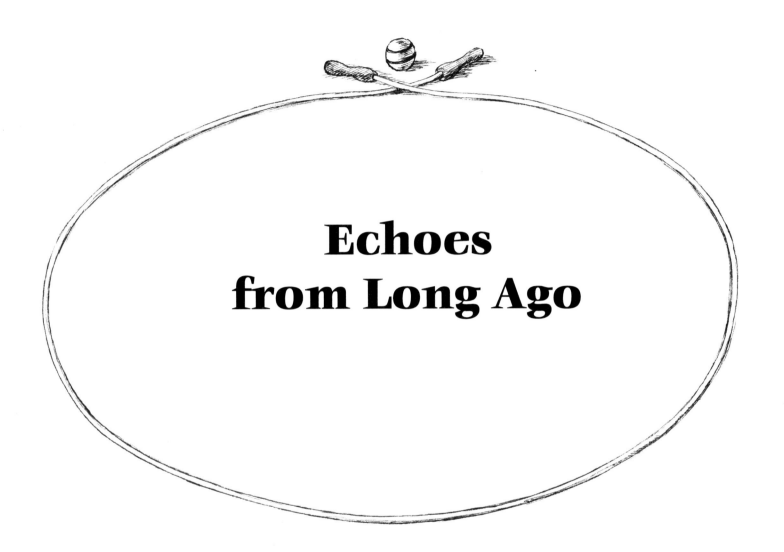

# Echoes
# from Long Ago

... woman to her son did utter,

Go, my son, and shut the shutter.

The shutter's shut, the son did utter,

I cannot shut it any shutter.

There was a man called Michael Finigan,
He grew whiskers on his chinigin,
He shaved them off but they grew in ag'in,
Poor old Michael Finigan, begin ag'in.

The wind, the wind, the wind blows high,
The snow comes falling from the sky,
Mary Thomson says she'll die
If she doesn't get a fellow with a roving eye.

54

*Round and round and round she goes,*
*And where she stops, nobody knows.*
*Point to the east, point to the west,*
*Point to the one that you love the best.*

The doggie will not bite you, nor you, nor you... but you!

Queen Anne, Queen Anne sits in her sedan,
Fair as a lily, white as a swan,
A pair of white gloves are over her hands
And she is the fairest in all the land.
Buy my lilies, buy my roses,
Make them into pretty posies
For the maiden you will choose.

picked it up, And put it in his pocket, P-O-C-K-E-T, pocket.

As I went up the ecky pecky road, I met a scabby donkey.

You one it, you two it,
You three it, you four it,
You five it, you six it,
You seven it, you ATE it!

One, two, three, four,
Mary at the kitchen door.
Five, six, seven, eight,
Mary at the garden gate.

**Stockings red,
garters blue,
Trimmed all round
with silver,
A red, red rose
upon my head,
And a gold ring
on my finger.
Tell me, tell me,
where I was born,
Over the hills
among the green corn.
A B C D E F G H I J K ...**

A
B
C
D
E
F
G
H
I
J K
L M
N
O
P Q
R
S
T
U
W V
X
Z Y

When Barney-boy was one, he learned to suck his thumb. Over Barney, over Barney, half past one. When Barney-boy was two, he learned to tie his shoe. Over Barney, over Barney, half past two. When Barney-boy was three, he always touched his knee. Over Barney, over Barney, half past three. When Barney-boy was four, he always touched the floor. Over Barney, over Barney, half past four. When Barney-boy was five, he learned to wink his eye. Over Barney, over Barney, half past five. When Barney-boy was six, he helped to pick up sticks. Over Barney, over Barney, half past six. When Barney-boy was seven, he watched the stars in heaven. Over Barney, over Barney, half past seven. When Barney-boy was eight, he always shut the gate. Over Barney, over Barney, half past eight. When Barney-boy was nine, he had a porcupine. Over Barney, over Barney, half past nine. When Barney-boy was ten, his pet it was a hen. Over Barney, over Barney, half past ten. When Barney-boy was eleven, he took a trip to Devon. Over Barney, over Barney, half past eleven. When Barney-boy was twelve, he learned to make a shelf. Over Barney, over Barney, half past twelve. When Barney-boy was grown, he sat upon a throne. Over Barney, over Barney, over Barney-boy!

On the mountain stands a lady,
Who she is I do not know.
All she wants is gold and silver,
All she wants is a nice young man.

**Lady, lady, touch the ground,**
**Lady, lady, turn right round;**
**Lady, lady, show your shoe,**
**Lady, lady, run right through.**

little shop. What do you sell? Ginger pop. How many bottles do you sell in a day? Twenty-four.

Now go away!

Water, water, wallflowers,
growing up so high,
We are all maidens
and we must all die,
Except for Nellie Ritchie,
the youngest of us all,
She can dance
and she can sing,
And she can do
the Highland Fling.
Fly, fly, fly for shame,
Turn your back
and look again!

Now you are married
we wish you joy,
First a girl
and then a boy,
Seven years after,
a son and a daughter,
Pray, young couple,
come kiss together,
Kiss her once,
kiss her twice,
Kiss her three times over.

SOAP

59

No more pencils, no more books,
No more teachers' ugly looks,
No more things that bring us sorrow
'Cos we won't be here tomorrow.

Davy, Davy, fie for shame,
Kissed the girls in a railway train.

Charlie, Charlie, chuck, chuck, chuck,
Went to bed with three young ducks.

Davy, Davy,
Stick him in the gravy.

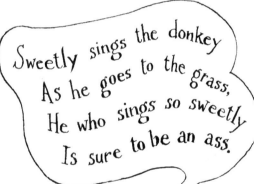

Sweetly sings the donkey
As he goes to the grass,
He who sings so sweetly
Is sure to be an ass.

Bobby, Bobby, number nine,
Sewed his breeks with binder twine.

Made you look, made you cry,
Made you buy a penny pie.
Look up, Look down,
You're the biggest
fool in town.

Adam and Eve and Pinch Me Tight
Went down to the sea to bathe.
Adam and Eve were drowned —
Which of the three was saved?

Georgie Porgie, pudding and pie,
Kissed the girls and made them cry,
When the boys came out to play,
Georgie Porgie ran away.

Dan, Dan, the dirty old man,
Washed his face in a frying pan.

Pinkety, pinkety,
Thumb to thumb,
Wish a wish and it's sure to come.
If yours comes true,
Mine will come true,
Pinkety, pinkety,
Thumb to thumb.

White horse,
white horse,
Bring me good luck.
Good luck to you,
Good luck to me,
Good luck to
everyone I see.

See a pin and pick it up,
All the day you'll have good luck.
See a pin and let it lay,
Bad luck you'll have all that day.

A dimple in your chin,
Your fortune will come in;
A dimple in your cheek,
Your fortune's far to seek.

MAGPIES

One for sorrow,
Two for mirth,
Three for a wedding,
Four for a birth.

Once upon a time when birds ate lime
And monkeys chewed tobacco,
The pigs took snuff to make them tough
And that's the end of the matter.

One midsummer's
night in winter
The snow was
raining fast,
A bare-footed girl
with clogs on
Stood sitting
on the grass.

I went to the pictures next Tuesday
And took a front seat at the back.
I said to the lady behind me,
I cannot see over your hat.
She gave me some well-broken biscuits,
I ate them and gave her them back;
I fell from the pit to the gallery
And broke my front bone at the back.

Last night,
the night before,
A lemon and a pickle
came knocking at my
door;
I went down
to let them in,
They hit me on the
head with a rolling
pin.

# Other Collections of Schoolyard Rhymes

Cole, Joanna, ed. *Anna Banana: 101 Jump-Rope Rhymes.* New York: Morrow Junior Books, 1989

Cole, Joanna, and Calmenson, Stephanie, eds. *Miss Mary Mack and Other Children's Street Rhymes.* New York: Morrow Junior Books, 1990

Delamar, Gloria T. *Children's Counting-Out Rhymes, Fingerplays, Jump-Rope and Bounce-Ball Chants and Other Rhythms.* Jefferson, NC: McFarland and Co., 1983

Fowke, Edith, ed. *Sally Go Round the Sun.* Toronto: McClelland & Stewart, 1969

Fraser, Amy Steward, ed. *Dae Ye Min' Langsyne? A Pot-pourri of Games, Rhymes and Ploys of Scottish Childhood.* London: Routledge & Kegan Paul, 1975

Gomme, Alice B. *The Traditional Games of England, Scotland, and Ireland.* 2 vols. New York: Dover, 1964

Greenaway, Kate. *Kate Greenaway's Book of Games.* New York: St. Martin's Press, 1987

Grugeon, Elizabeth. "Children's Oral Culture: A Transitional Experience." In *Oracy Matters: The Development of Talking and Listening in Education,* edited by Margaret MacLure, Terry Phillips and Andrew Wilkinson. Milton Keynes, England: Open University Press, 1988

Kane, Alice. *Songs and Sayings of an Ulster Childhood.* Toronto: McClelland & Stewart, 1983

Knapp, Herbert, and Knapp, Mary. *One Potato, Two Potato ... The Secret Education of American Children.* New York: W.W. Norton, 1976

Milnes, Gerald. *Granny, Will Your Dog Bite and Other Mountain Rhymes.* New York: Alfred A. Knopf, 1990

Opie, Iona and Peter. *Children's Games in Street and Playground.* New York: Oxford University Press, 1984

Opie, Iona and Peter, eds. *I Saw Esau: The Schoolchild's Pocket Book.* Cambridge, MA: Candlewick Press, 1992

Opie, Iona and Peter. *The Lore and Language of School Children.* London: Oxford University Press, 1989

Peer, Willie van. "Counting Out: Form and Function of Children's Counting-Out Rhymes." In *Oracy Matters: The Development of Talking and Listening in Education,* edited by Margaret MacLure, Terry Phillips and Andrew Wilkinson. Milton Keynes, England: Open University Press, 1988

Pierce, Maggi Kerr. *Keep the Kettle Boiling: Rhymes from a Belfast Childhood.* Belfast: Appletree Press, 1983

Rosen, Michael, and Steele, Susanna, eds. *Inky Pinky Ponky: Children's Playground Rhymes.* London: Collins Picture Lions, 1982

Skolnik, Peter L. *Jump Rope!* New York: Workman Publishing Co., 1974

Withers, Carl, ed. *I Saw a Rocket Walk a Mile.* New York: Holt Rinehart and Winston, 1965

Withers, Carl, ed. *A Rocket in My Pocket: The Rhymes and Chants of Young Americans.* New York: Henry Holt, 1948

Yolen, Jane, ed. *Street Rhymes Around the World.* Homesdale, PA: Wordsong, Boyd Mills Press, 1992

Zola, Meguido, ed. *By Hook or By Crook: My Autograph Book.* Montreal: Tundra Books, 1987

# Index of First Lines

A E I O U, 14
Adam and Eve and Pinch Me Tight, 63
Are you coming out, sir? 34
As I climbed up the apple tree, 6
As I sat under the apple tree, 38
As I went up the ecky pecky road, 56
Ask no questions, 37

Billy gave me apples, 9
Birds of a feather flock together, 37
Bluebells, cockle shells, 8
Bobby, Bobby, number nine, 62

Charley went over the ocean, 12
Charlie Chaplin went to France, 31
Charlie, Charlie, chuck, chuck, chuck, 62
Chester, have you heard about Harry, 10
Cinderella dressed in yella, 8
Cinderelli, dressed in yelli, 32

Dan, Dan, the dirty old man, 63
Davy, Davy, 62
Davy, Davy, fie for shame, 62
Deck the halls with poison ivy, 19
A dimple in your chin, 65
Doctor Knickerbocker, 5
The doggie will not bite you, 55
Down in the meadow, 33
Down in the valley, 61

Each peach, pear, plum, 8
Eatum, peatum, potum, pye, 54
Eeka locka, 13
Eenie, meenie, minie, mo, 34
The elephant is a pretty bird, 38

Fireman, fireman, number eight, 35
A fly and a flea flew up in a flue, 41
Four more days and we are free, 46
The funniest thing I've ever seen, 29

Georgie Porgie, pudding and pie, 63
Give me five, 4

Ha! ha! ha! He! he! he! 37
Had a little sports car 298, viii
Happy birthday to you, Smashed tomatoes, 11

Happy birthday to you, You live, 11
Here comes the teacher yelling, 33
Hey, Peter! 13
Hickory, dickory, 12
Hot-cross buns, 6
Hot potato, pass it on, 9
How much wood would a
   woodchuck chuck, 41

I eat my peas with honey, 42
I hear you say I say I say, 40
I saw you in the ocean, 25
I scream, you scream, 6
I sent a letter to my love, 54
I went into the house, 20
I went to the pictures next Tuesday, 67
I woke up Sunday morning, 7
If Peter Piper picked, 41
If you sneeze on Monday, 17
If you think you are in love, 22
I'm a little acorn brown, 2
I'm a little sandy girl, 54
I'm a raindrop, 11
I'm Chiquita Banana, 46
I'm rubber, you're glue, 36

Jingle bells, 18
Jonathan and Alexandra, 10
Julius Caesar, 43

Ladies and gentlemen, 38
Ladles and Jellyspoons, 60
Lady, lady, touch the ground, 58
Last night, the night before, 67

Made you look, made you cry, 63
Mary had a little cow, 27
Mary had a little lamb, Her father, 26
Mary had a little lamb, It was, 27
Mary had a little lamb, Its fleece, 26
Mary had a little lamb, You've heard, 27
Mickey Mouse Built a house, 8
Mind your own business, 25
Miss Mary had a steamboat, 16
Miss Mary Mack, Mack, Mack, vi
Monkey in the jailhouse, 35

Mother, may I take a swim? 29
Motorboat, motorboat, go so slow, 32
My boyfriend's name is Addie, 14
My mother wanted peaches, 44

No more pencils ... dirty looks, 19
No more pencils ... here tomorrow, 61
Nobody likes me, 39
Now you are married we wish you joy, 59

Oh say can you see, 36
Old John Tucker was a mighty man, 11
On the mountain stands a lady ... new
   friend, 4
On the mountain stands a lady ... young
   man, 58
On the mountain stands a school, 32
Once upon a time when birds ate lime, 66
One for sorrow, two for joy, 50
One for sorrow, Two for mirth, 65
One midsummer's night in winter, 66
One, two, three, four ... cottage door, 13
One, two, three, four ... kitchen door, 56
Over the lake, 12

A peanut sat on the railway track, 43
Pepsi-Cola went to town, 42
Peter, Peter, if you're able, 3
Pigs like mud, 2
Pinkety, pinkety, thumb to thumb, 64
Popeye the sailor man, 42
Postman, postman, 22
Pounds, shillings, pence, 61

Queen Anne, Queen Anne, 55
Quick, quick, 60

Rick chick ma ma, 4
Roger and Debbie, 36
Roses are red, Cabbages, 36
Roses are red, Violets, 24
Round and round and round she goes, 55
Row, row, row your boat, 18

Salome was a dancer, 44
See a pin and pick it up, 65
Step in a hole, 17
Sticks and stones may break my bones, 37

Stockings red, garters blue, 56
Sweetly sings the donkey, 62

Tarzan, Tarzan, in the air, 25
Teacher, teacher, we don't care, 47
There was a man called Michael Finigan, 52
This is the way you spell Tennessee, 34
Three-six-nine! 36
Through the teeth, 24
A tisket, a tasket, 54
Tom, Tom, the piper's son, 18
Tonight, tonight, the pillow fight, 46

Up on the housetop, reindeer pause, 18

Up the river, 46

Vegetable Love, 23

Water, water, wallflowers, 59
Way down south where bananas grow, 28
What's the time? A minute, 30
What's the time? About, 30
What's the time? Half past kissing, 30
What's the time? Half past, quarter, 30
What's the time? Ten o'clock, 30
What's the time? The same, 30
What's the time? Time you bought, 30
What's the time? Time you knew, 30

What's your name? 58
When Barney-boy was one, 57
When I eat my Smarties, 2
When you fall in the river, 22
When you get married, 25
When you see a monkey up a tree, 24
White horse, white horse, 64
Who stole the cookie from the cookie jar? 30
The wind, the wind, the wind blows high, 53
A woman to her son did utter, 52
The wonder ball, 15

You can fall from a steeple, 53

# Index of Rhymes by Type

**ACTION RHYMES**
Charley went over the ocean, 12
Doctor Knickerbocker, 5
Give me five, 4
Miss Mary Mack, Mack, Mack, vi
My boyfriend's name is Addie, 14
My mother wanted peaches, 44
On the mountain stands a lady ... new
    friend, 4
Up on the housetop, reindeer pause, 18
When Barney-boy was one, 57

**AUTOGRAPH VERSES**
As I sat under the apple tree, 38
Birds of a feather flock together, 37
The elephant is a pretty bird, 38
Ha! ha! ha! He! he! he! 37
I saw you in the ocean, 25
Mind your own business, 25
Oh say can you see, 36
On the mountain stands a lady ... young
    man, 58
Roger and Debbie, 36
Roses are red, Cabbages, 36
Roses are red, Violets, 24
Tarzan, Tarzan, in the air, 25
Through the teeth, 24

When you get married, 25
When you see a monkey up a tree, 24
The wind, the wind, the wind blows high, 53
You can fall from a steeple, 53

**BALL-BOUNCE CHANTS**
Are you coming out, sir? 34
As I went up the ecky pecky road, 56
Billy gave me apples, 9
Charlie Chaplin went to France, 31
Cinderella dressed in yella, 8
Cinderelli, dressed in yelli, 32
Down in the meadow, 33
Had a little sports car 298, viii
Here comes the teacher yelling, 33
Lady, lady, touch the ground, 58
Mickey Mouse Built a house, 8
On the mountain stands a school, 32
One, two, three, four ... kitchen door, 56
Stockings red, garters blue, 56
This is the way you spell Tennessee, 34
Water, water, wallflowers, 59
When Barney-boy was one, 57

**CALL-AND-RESPONSE RHYMES**
Are you coming out, sir? 34
I went into the house, 20

Rick chick ma ma, 4
What's the time? A minute, 30
What's the time? About, 30
What's the time? Half past kissing, 30
What's the time? Half past, quarter, 30
What's the time? Ten o'clock, 30
What's the time? The same, 30
What's the time? Time you bought, 30
What's the time? Time you knew, 30
Who stole the cookie from the cookie jar? 30

**COUNTING-OUT RHYMES**
A E I O U, 14
As I climbed up the apple tree, 6
The doggie will not bite you, 55
Eatum, peatum, potum, pye, 54
Eeka locka, 13
Eenie, meenie, minie, mo, 34
Fireman, fireman, number eight, 35
Hey, Peter! 13
Hickory, dickory, 12
Hot-cross buns, 6
Hot potato, pass it on, 9
I sent a letter to my love, 54
I woke up Sunday morning, 7
I'm a little sandy girl, 54
Monkey in the jailhouse, 35

Old John Tucker was a mighty man, 11
One, two, three, four ... cottage door, 13
Over the lake, 12
Queen Anne, Queen Anne, 55
Round and round and round she goes, 55
A tisket, a tasket, 54
The wonder ball, 15

**NONSENSE VERSES**

As I sat under the apple tree, 38
The elephant is a pretty bird, 38
The funniest thing I've ever seen, 29
I eat my peas with honey, 42
I scream, you scream, 6
I went to the pictures next Tuesday, 67
I woke up Sunday morning, 7
I'm a little acorn brown, 2
Ladles and Jellyspoons, 60
Last night, the night before, 67
Mary had a little cow, 27
Mary had a little lamb, Her father, 26
Mary had a little lamb, It was, 27
Mary had a little lamb, Its fleece, 26
Mary had a little lamb, You've heard, 27
Mother, may I take a swim? 29
Once upon a time when birds ate lime, 66
One midsummer's night in winter, 66
A peanut sat on the railway track, 43
Pepsi-Cola went to town, 42
Popeye the sailor man, 42
Quick, quick, 60
Tarzan, Tarzan, in the air, 25
There was a man called Michael Finigan, 52
Through the teeth, 24
Way down south where bananas grow, 28
When I eat my Smarties, 2

**ROMANCE RHYMES**

If you think you are in love, 22
My boyfriend's name is Addie, 14
Pigs like mud, 2
Postman, postman, 22
Vegetable Love, 23
When you fall in the river, 22
The wind, the wind, the wind blows high, 53
You can fall from a steeple, 53

**SCHOOL RHYMES**

Down in the valley, 61
Four more days and we are free, 46

I'm Chiquita Banana, 46
No more pencils ... dirty looks, 19
No more pencils ... here tomorrow, 61
Pounds, shillings, pence, 61
Row, row, row your boat, 18
Teacher, teacher, we don't care, 47
Tom, Tom, the piper's son, 18
Tonight, tonight, the pillow fight, 46
Up the river, 46

**SKIPPING SONGS**

Billy gave me apples, 9
Bluebells, cockle shells, 8
Cinderella dressed in yella, 8
Cinderelli, dressed in yelli, 32
Down in the meadow, 33
Each peach, pear, plum, 8
Had a little sports car 298, viii
Here comes the teacher yelling, 33
Lady, lady, touch the ground, 58
Mickey Mouse Built a house, 8
Motorboat, motorboat, go so slow, 32
Now you are married we wish you joy, 59
On the mountain stands a lady ... new friend, 4
On the mountain stands a lady ... young
   man, 58
On the mountain stands a school, 32
Stockings red, garters blue, 56
What's your name? 58

**SUPERSTITIONS**

A dimple in your chin, 65
If you sneeze on Monday, 17
One for sorrow, two for joy, 50
One for sorrow, Two for mirth, 65
Pinkety, pinkety, thumb to thumb, 64
See a pin and pick it up, 65
Step in a hole, 17
White horse, white horse, 64

**TAUNTS AND TEASES**

Adam and Eve and Pinch Me Tight, 63
As I went up the ecky pecky road, 56
Ask no questions, 37
Birds of a feather flock together, 37
Bobby, Bobby, number nine, 62
Charlie, Charlie, chuck, chuck, chuck, 62

Chester, have you heard about Harry, 10
Dan, Dan, the dirty old man, 63
Davy, Davy, 62
Davy, Davy, fie for shame, 62
Deck the halls with poison ivy, 19
Down in the valley, 61
Four more days and we are free, 46
Georgie Porgie, pudding and pie, 63
Ha! ha! ha! He! he! he! 37
Happy birthday to you, Smashed tomatoes, 11
Happy birthday to you, You live, 11
I saw you in the ocean, 25
I went into the house, 20
I'm a raindrop, 11
I'm Chiquita Banana, 46
I'm rubber, you're glue, 36
Jingle bells, 18
Jonathan and Alexandra, 10
Julius Caesar, 43
Ladies and gentlemen, 38
Made you look, made you cry, 63
Mind your own business, 25
Miss Mary had a steamboat, 16
No more pencils ... dirty looks, 19
Nobody likes me, 39
Oh say can you see, 36
Peter, Peter, if you're able, 3
Roger and Debbie, 36
Roses are red, Cabbages, 36
Roses are red, Violets, 24
Row, row, row your boat, 18
Salome was a dancer, 44
Sticks and stones may break my bones, 37
Sweetly sings the donkey, 62
Teacher, teacher, we don't care, 47
Three-six-nine! 36
Tom, Tom, the piper's son, 18
When you get married, 25
When you see a monkey up a tree, 24

**TONGUE TWISTERS**

A fly and a flea flew up in a flue, 41
How much wood would a
   woodchuck chuck, 41
I hear you say I say I say, 40
If Peter Piper picked, 41
A woman to her son did utter, 52

Book design and type by N.R. Jackson
Set in Veljovic type
Hand lettering done by the artist
Maryann Kovalski's illustrations are a combination of
historic nineteenth-century woodcuts and pen-and-ink drawings
on Arches medium tooth paper.

Film by Bergman Graphics Limited
Printed and bound in Hong Kong by
Wing King Tong Company Limited